CANADA · AT · WORK

Mining

Written by Jane Drake with Ann Love
Illustrated by Pat Cupples

Kids Can Press

"Your hockey coach says we've raised enough money to go to the Junior Miner's Tournament in Edmonton," Dad tells the twins. "You'll play teams from all over the country."

"Wow! Can I get new skates?" Jamie asks, unpacking his equipment bag.

"Your skates still fit," Mom says. "Besides, skates don't grow on trees. Think of all the things that go into making them. Leather, plastic, steel …"

2

"Steel just comes from a factory, doesn't it?" asks Trish.

"Actually, it all starts with minerals and metals found in rock in the ground," Mom explains. "Like the nickel at the mine where I work."

"No way," says Jamie.

"Why don't you come and see for yourself?" suggests Mom.

"Then I'll take you to the steel mill where nickel is added to iron ore to make the steel tough enough for skate blades," offers Dad.

"Cool!" the twins shout together.

3

Driving to the mine, Mom explains that it takes a lot of people, money and time to develop a mine. Mining companies use special equipment — even satellites — to look for clues above and below the earth's surface that help them detect valuable minerals hidden underground. If they find a large deposit, and get government permission, they may start a mine.

aerial survey plane

4

boring drill

"Those workers over there are geologists," Mom says. "They are drilling holes that go down farther than the CN Tower goes up. If they're lucky, the rock samples, or core segments, they bring to the surface will show signs of minerals — such as gold, nickel or iron."

"How did the minerals get there?" asks Trish.

"By chance," Mom explains. "As Earth formed and changed over millions of years, different minerals were trapped in rocks."

core segments

5

Trish's and Jamie's ears pop as the elevator heads down the mine shaft. It's damp, warm and breezy below ground — but most of all, it's dark. Tunnels branch off the shaft, and work crews are busy all over the mine.

headframe

elevator shaft

ventilation shaft

elevator

Why is it so windy down here?

The air is circulated, just like it is in a house. Fumes and dust are removed and the humidity is controlled. In winter, we heat parts of the mine, too.

underground machine shop

In years past, only strong men had jobs in mines. Women were not allowed. Now machines do most of the work, operated by women, men and computers. For safety, miners work in groups. Everyone must be fit and properly trained to operate the complicated machinery.

crusher

ling ore

drilling

skip

loading ore

skip shaft

installing safety nets

mine cart

Mine walls are made of a mixture of rock and minerals called ore. The variety of minerals and their colours and textures make each wall different. A wall that contains metals may glitter and sparkle. Nickel ore can be many colours, from grey and black to a shiny gold.

Where there is a rich vein of ore, workers use drilling machines to drill holes in the mine walls.

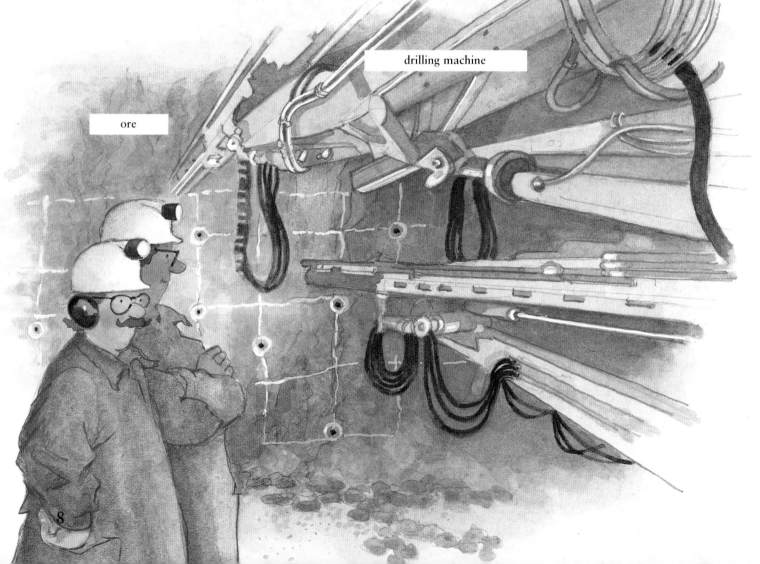

ore

drilling machine

8

Blasting experts fill the holes with explosives. When the mine is cleared of people, the team sets off a blast by remote control. Then, heavy-duty vehicles haul the ore to an underground crushing station. The crushed ore is transported to the surface.

"How does it get there?" Jamie yells over the noise of the machinery.

"In a special elevator called a skip," shouts Mom.

explosives

On the surface, an enormous crusher smashes the ore into smaller pieces. Conveyor belts deliver the crushed ore to a nearby concentrating mill. There the valuable metal will be separated from the worthless rock called gangue.

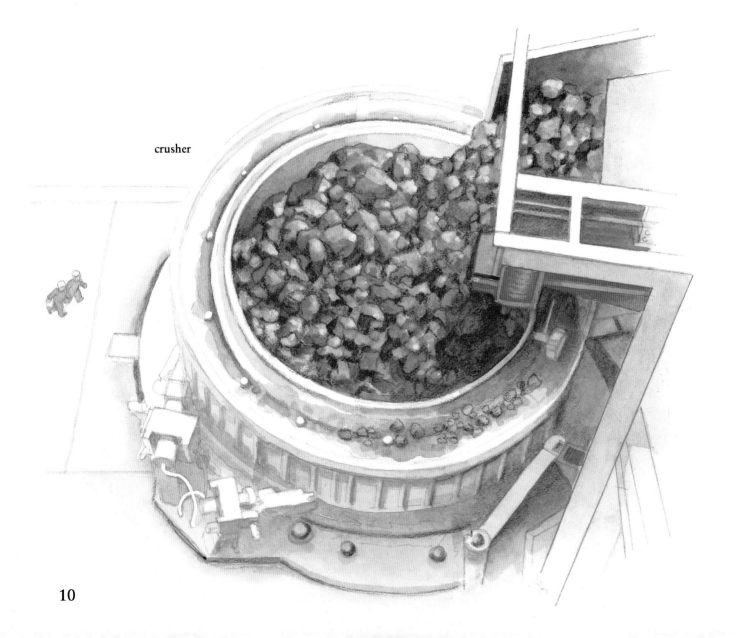

crusher

At this concentrating mill, machines grind nickel ore to a fine powder. In big tubs called flotation cells, the powder is combined with water and chemicals to make a gritty pulp. Air is forced through the mixture, trapping bits of nickel in bubbles floating on the surface. The gangue falls to the bottom.

"At a smelter, the bits of nickel ore are heated and refined to form pellets of pure nickel," Mom tells them. "These pellets go by truck to a steel mill, like the one where Dad works."

grinding machine

Hey! It looks like metal. Is it steel yet?

No. Iron is the main ingredient in steel. But nickel is added to make a special type of steel that is shiny, hard and stainless. That means no rust.

At the steel mill, iron ore pellets are put in a huge blast furnace with limestone and fuel called coke. When the furnace is hot, the coke burns and the iron ore and limestone melt. The liquid iron sinks to the bottom of the furnace. The liquid limestone floats to the top and traps bits of impure iron. This waste, called slag, is collected for disposal.

blast furnace

making ingots

The liquid iron is heated again in another kind of furnace where the nickel pellets can be added to make stainless steel. This liquid steel is ladled into moulds called ingots. The ingots are heated again and made into bars, beams, plates and sheets.

"Regular steel is shipped to factories to make such goods as cars and refrigerators. Stainless steel is made into products such as kitchen sinks and cutlery," Dad tells them. "And skate blades of course," he adds.

making a sheet of steel

rolled sheets of stainless steel

13

On the way to Edmonton, the twins take turns at the airplane window, peppering their parents with questions. They've flown for hours over forests, lakes and prairie fields.

"Are there any mines down there?" Jamie asks.

"There are many kinds of mines all across Canada," Mom explains. "Some are underground and others are open-pit mines on the surface. Before the tournament we're going to visit an oil mine that is above ground."

Driving north from the airport, Dad explains that oil was
formed in dinosaur times. Dead plants and animals fell to
the sea floor, were squashed under layers of mud, and
eventually became oil. Some of that oil was trapped in
underground pools. Geologists look for oil pools
using underground computer pictures. When
they find a big pool, an oil company may
drill a well and pump the oil from
the ground.

oil pump

shale

limestone

gas

oil

water

"Oil can also be found mixed with sand, water and clay," Dad tells them. "This is called oil sand and it's easy to find. Look at that riverbank. The gummy black sand is bubbling right out of the ground."

"How can you mine oily sand?" asks Trish.

"That's what we're going to see. My first engineering job was here in Alberta's oil sands."

oil sand

Special mining machines were designed for the oil sands. A dragline excavator throws its gigantic scoop into the mine pit, drags it back full of oil sand, and dumps its load in a pile. Specially trained operators work with computers to make sure the dragline runs smoothly.

dragline excavator

conveyor belt

Another huge machine, called a bucketwheel, moves the oil sand from the pile onto a conveyor belt that carries the oil sand to the separation plant. There are 50 kilometres (30 miles) of conveyor belts in this mine.

bucketwheel

In the separation plant, the oil sand goes into enormous revolving machines called tumblers. Hot water, chemicals and steam are added, and the mixture is tumbled like clothes in a dryer. Then it is poured into a big open vat where the gritty oil froths to the surface as foam and most of the sand and clay sink to the bottom. The foamy oil is skimmed off and put into a gigantic spinning machine called a centrifuge.

"How does a centrifuge work?" asks Jamie.

"Like a salad spinner. The oil spins out, leaving behind more bits of sand and clay."

tumbler

Finally, the oil is superheated in a coking furnace — a huge oven where the oil separates into coke, sulphur, crude oil and gas. Coke is used to fuel the oven and sulphur is sold for fertilizer. Crude oil and gas must be refined before they can be used.

"What does 'superheated' mean?" pipes up Trish.

"It means the furnace temperature is 550°C (1022°F)," replies Dad. "That's hotter than a firecracker."

coking furnace

Crude oil travels to refineries in steel pipelines. Most pipes are buried about 2 metres (6½ feet) underground, where the temperature is steady. Pipes above the ground are warmed in winter so the oil will flow. Pumping stations along the pipeline keep the oil moving. Computers control the flow of oil and check for leaks.

oil refinery

laying a pipeline

holding tanks for oil

At the refinery, the oil is heated again. When the oil boils, it can be separated into gasoline for cars, diesel fuel for trucks or tractors, and heating oil for homes. Tanker trucks, rail tankers, ocean tankers and more pipelines carry these oil products across the country and around the world. Oil-refinery leftovers are turned into grease for lubricating machinery and asphalt for paving roads.

tanker truck

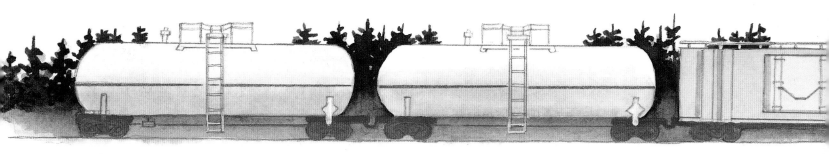

rail tanker

ocean tanker

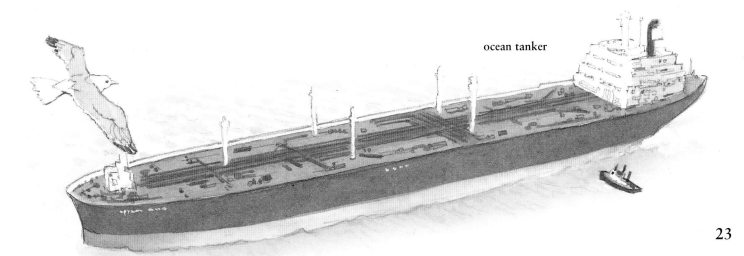

23

Most refined oil is burned as fuel to create energy.
Energy makes it possible to heat buildings, freeze ice, light
streets and power engines. But that's not all oil is used for.
Many things that don't look like oil are actually made
from oil. Petrochemical plants combine oil by-products
with chemicals to make paint, animal feed, medicine, glue,
explosives, detergents and plastics. Plastic is used to make
thousands of products — from carpets to goalie masks.
Using oil by-products saves money and reduces waste.

petrochemical refinery

For Trish and Jamie, mining provides jobs for their parents and makes their favourite game possible. But there's no stickhandling around the fact that mining causes pollution.

Mining always changes the environment. When minerals and oil are removed from the ground, plant life and wildlife are either disturbed or destroyed. And the minerals and oil can never be replaced. They don't regrow the way trees do.

NO DUMPING

Refining and milling cause air and water pollution. The furnaces and machines use a lot of energy and create toxic smoke that harms the atmosphere. The enormous quantities of fresh water that are mixed with oil sand or ore become unsafe for people and wildlife. And accidents, such as oil spills, endanger habitats and wildlife.

People cause all these problems, but they can also control them.

oil-spill cleanup

"What happens to the leftover sand, Dad?" asks Trish.

"Mining of oil sands disturbs large areas that must be turned back into habitat for wildlife. Now, mine pits are being filled with leftover sand and planted with specially developed plants."

"Remember the gangue at the nickel mine and the slag at the steel mill? What about all that waste?" Jamie asks.

"Slag and gangue are mixed with cement and used to backfill mine tunnels after the ore has been removed," Dad explains. "Mining waste used to be dumped in ugly, lifeless piles called slag heaps. It took years of research to find plants that would grow in these places. Now slag heaps are being turned into places where plants grow and wildlife can live."

People want governments to get tough with companies that pollute. But every person needs to help, by using mining products and fossil fuels with care. Think about the lights you use and the car rides you take. Learn to live by the four Rs: reduce, reuse, recycle and refuse.

recreation area on a reclaimed mine site

As the Zamboni prepares the ice for the first game of the tournament, Trish and Jamie look around the arena.

"I can see twenty-three things made from steel or oil," Jamie says.

"Did you count the ref's whistle? That makes twenty-four!" says Trish, pulling on her goalie mask. "Come on, let's play."

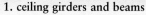

1. ceiling girders and beams
2. heating pipes
3. metal benches
4. Zamboni
5. fire alarm
6. metal roll-up door
7. metal face guards on helmets
8. exit sign
9. loudspeaker
10. net frame
11. metal guards on lights
12. clock and scoreboard
13. metal heaters above stands
14. ref's whistle
15. puck
16. plastic helmet
17. Plexiglas around rink
18. ice (cooled using energy)
19. hockey tape
20. plastic netting
21. garbage can
22. water bottles
23. plastic protectors — shin, shoulder, elbow pads
24. skate guards

Index

This book is dedicated to my hockey players, Brian, Steph and Moo — J.D.

The authors gratefully acknowledge the assistance of Gord Ball; Jane Crist; Jim, Stephanie, Brian and Madeline Drake; Tom and Cindy Drake; Ian Hamilton; Keith Hendrick; Robin Humphreys; Bob Keyes; Peter McBride; Johnnie Morrison; Fred Newton; Peter Newton; Deborah Nicely, Nordberg Inc. Global Mining Division; Ontario Mining Association; Ian Plummer; Tom Ryley; Bob Shaver; Mary and Doug Thompson; Aileen and Ken Thompson; Mrs. Potvin-Schafer's 3/4 class, Whitney Public School.

Thanks to Valerie Hussey, Ricky Englander and all the people at Kids Can Press. A special thank you to Pat Cupples, Debbie Rogosin and Trudee Romanek, who know that the best steel comes from the hottest fires.

Text © 1997 Jane Drake and Ann Love
Illustrations © 1997 Pat Cupples

Kids Can Press acknowledges the financial support of the Ontario Arts Council, the Canada Council for the Arts and the Government of Canada, through the BPIDP, for our publishing activity.

Kids Can Press Ltd.
29 Birch Avenue
Toronto, Ontario, Canada
M4V 1E2

The artwork in this book was rendered in watercolour, gouache, graphite and coloured pencils on hot-press watercolour paper.

Edited by Debbie Rogosin and Trudee Romanek
Designed by Marie Bartholomew and Karen Powers
Printed in China

The hardcover edition of this book is smyth sewn casebound.
The paperback edition of this book is limp sewn with a drawn-on cover.

CDN 97 0 9 8 7 6 5 4 3 2 1
CDN PA 01 0 9 8 7 6 5 4 3 2 1

Canadian Cataloguing in Publication Data

Drake, Jane
    Mining

(Canada at work)

Includes index.
ISBN 1-55074-337-6 (bound) ISBN 1-55074-920-X (pbk.)

1. Mining engineering — Juvenile literature. 2. Mineral industries — Juvenile literature. 3. Mines and mineral resources — Juvenile literature. I. Love, Ann. II. Cupples, Patricia. III. Title. IV. Series.

TN148.D72 1997 j622 C96-932204-6

Kids Can Press is a Nelvana company